MOTHERHOOD IS NOT A REHEARSAL
Bottom-line Mentoring for Parents

by
Dr. Noya Ostrowiak

**"A mother understands what her
child doesn't say."**

Old proverb

Southern Charm Press, 150 Caldwell Drive, Hampton, GA 30228
Visit our Web site at www.southerncharmpress.com

The publisher offers discounts on this book when purchased in quantities. For more information, contact: toll free: 1-888-281-9393, fax: 770-946-5220, e-mail: info@southerncharmpress.com

Printed in the United States of America
First Printing: March 2001

Library of Congress Card Number
LCCN 00-109820

Ostrowiak, Noya Dr.
Motherhood Is Not A Rehearsal / Dr. Noya Ostrowiak

ISBN 0-9702190-4-0

Original painting by Dr. Noya Ostrowiak

Photographer of painting Jess Lacher

Dedication

To My Mother Miriam,
Orit and Tal my daughters,
with love

Acknowledgements

My gratitude to my husband Terry for his help and support.

To my daughters Orit and Tal for their trust and love.

A special note of thanks to my editor Dr.Robert Goodman from Silvercat, San Diego, for his care, interest and professional help and to my Publisher Kathy Williams for giving me this opportunity.

Author's biography

Dr. Noya Ostrowiak is a mother and a grandmother. She taught literature to high school kids in Israel and lectured at the University of South Africa.

She wrote a fiction book which was published in England.

In The Netherlands she obtained an M.A. degree in management and worked together with her husband, Terry, who is an International business coach.

Noya, her husband, her daughters and grandughter are now living in The United States of America.

Dear Mom,

I wish you a sky

If I could make a wish for you,
I would wish you a sky.
With colors so very bright and blue,
And a magic that flies.

Nothing is good enough for you,
So I wish you a sky,
Because there are no limits, true
And no borders too high.

Words cannot possibly express
My love for you inside.
It's only with this wish, I guess
That you can feel my pride.

So, now you understand what is meant when I say:
"If I could make a wish for you,
I would wish you a sky".

Love,
Orit

Table of Contents

1.
HOW IT ALL STARTED

The plane had just landed at San Diego airport and my journey of Twenty Four hours had finally come to an end. I was tired and drained. My dream was to stretch my sore limbs on my bed and close my eyes.

"Mom, Tal and I have a great idea," my daughter Orit announced excitedly after kissing me. "We want you to write a book about being a mother."

I looked at her, hardly managing to focus. "Right now I am too tired to even talk," was my reply to this unexpected request. "O.K. I understand. We'll talk about it tomorrow," she said.

"Mom, will you do it?" was the first thing she asked me when she phoned the following morning. "Do what?" I wanted to know, completely forgetting her question from the previous day.

"Write about motherhood."

"What is there to write about? It's all so obvious," I said, wishing to end the discussion.

"Whatever you say Mom. By the way, I plan on going to the shop, do you need anything for the house?" She was quick to change the subject.

I was grateful for the offer and gave her a list of items I needed. When I put down the phone, I was sure that I had managed to get out of this assignment. Ten minutes later the phone rang again. This time my daughter Tal was on the line. She wasted no time before saying that Orit and she would like their children to have a childhood similar to theirs. So, would I please agree to write some guidelines on motherhood for the two of them?

"We know from our own experience that whatever you write is not just theory. It would not be something written, using the word 'you' instead of 'I' to tell others how they should act. What you write is what you actually did, and we know that it works — it worked for us. And, she added, "maybe others will also enjoy reading your thoughts."

I thanked her for the compliment. I said that I needed time to think about it and that I wouldn't even know how to begin. I was still hoping to get out of it. "You'll find a way Mom. We are not asking you to write a cook book," she added, humoring me, because she knew how limited my knowledge of that subject was.

The following days, while battling jet lag, I found myself jotting down all the ideas and thoughts that came to my mind. I was surprised at what I came up with.

The next time I spoke to my daughters, I said that I would do it on one condition — that they also participate in the process. I still hoped for a way out! Without any hesitation, they both agreed.

I hope that my daughters will find what they are looking for in the following pages — and maybe others will too

BOTTOM LINE:

**"What you write, is what you actually did, and we know that it works — it worked for us. And maybe others will also enjoy reading your thoughts."
— Orit and Tal.**

2.

WHY DO WE WANT TO HAVE CHILDREN?

At a certain point in my life, I couldn't wait to have a child. I was ready to be a mother, and I knew why I wanted children.

Come to think about it, why do we want to be parents? When I get a car, for instance, I know why I want it — primarily to get around. I also know that it needs looking after; it needs to be cleaned, serviced, registered, and insured. There is a whole book of instructions that tells me what a car is and what it needs. Although a car is just "a thing," I still have a "relationship" with it. So if I know why I want a car, which is just a thing, and if I am aware of what I commit to when I buy a car, surely, before I give life to a child, I should know and understand why I want a child and what is involved!

Having children should not be a matter of "Oh, well, I just fell pregnant." We shouldn't just "fall" or "get" pregnant; it must not be a "by the way" affair. This is not a game that we unconsciously get involved in.

We are bringing a new life into the world, a life that will become our full responsibility. If we do not understand this to start with, how will we handle it later?

We must make a conscious decision, one that we give serious thought to.

Finding the answer to the "why," clarifies that having a child fulfills *our* needs, not the needs of the "planned/not yet existent" child.

Whatever our reason, the bottom line is that we want a child to satisfy our self-ish needs.

Over the years I asked various parents why they had children. Many of them looked at me in astonishment. "What kind of a question is this?" they answered with a question. When I repeated the question, most said they never thought about it. "You just have kids, that's how it is," was a common reply.

Some said it was because their parents or society expected them to, or because all their friends had kids.

Other replies included:

— they were following the natural instinct of having offspring;

— they desired to leave a mark on the world;

— they felt a need to nurture;

— they wanted to fulfill the need to create;

— they loved kids;

— they wished to re-live their childhood;

— they wanted to offset the sense of deprivation they had as children.

One mother bluntly said that she wanted kids to ensure that someone would look after her in old age. "And having just two children isn't enough," she went on. "I want four kids so that they will be able to share this duty."

We can change or replace a car because we don't like the color any longer or because it's too old or just because we feel like a change, but we must always remember that we can never change or replace a child!

As a mother and parent, I committed myself to taking full responsibility for my child's physical, emotional, and mental well-being. I can't be a mother one day and stop the next just because it doesn't suit me any longer!

Some people tire quickly from things and from other people, including their own spouses, and are forever busy changing the world around them. Whatever they do to calm their inner restlessness, they must always remember that they can't do it with a child, or to a child. It is not a game; we are not playing with dolls!

BOTTOM LINE:

When we are ready to become mothers and parents, we need to understand why we want children in our lives and that we are taking on a lifetime commitment.

3

WE ARE RESPONSIBLE FOR OUR "SELF" AND OUR CHILD'S "SELF"

Whatever our reason for becoming parents, the decision to have a child is ours. We decide for ourselves and for them. Our children didn't ask us to be born.

We are about to embark on a lifetime relationship between people, without asking the other partners in this relationship if they even want to be part of it.

When we bring a life into the world, we commit ourselves to taking full responsibility; we do not do the child a favor by becoming parents.

To say to a child, "I sacrificed my life for you," to present a child with a list of all that we did for him or her, is one of the greatest sins a parent can commit. In fact it is emotional abuse and blackmail! It's a reminder that the child is indebted to us. It tells the child that "because I am your parent, you owe me now and forever." It communicates dissatisfaction with the way the child "repays" the debt. It blames the child for the parent's unhappiness or lack of fulfillment. It holds the child responsible for making the parent lose out in life. Emotionally it shackles and cripples the child.

Do we want our child to say: "What do you expect of me? Whatever I do is never good enough for you. What am I repaying you for? I didn't ask you to be born!"

The woman who wanted to become a mother in order to have children to look after her when she got old placed great expectations on her children. She knew how her children were supposed to repay her in the future. They owed her, even before they were born.

And what if they were unable to repay her the way she planned? Would she then present them with the list of her "good deeds" for which they were indebted?

This isn't fair!

Declarations of sacrifice cause the child to feel inadequate, guilty, and resentful and, as time passes, to view the parents as a heavy burden.

In our relations with our kids, we don't need to list "what we did for the child." It's better to leave the "lists" for our shopping at the supermarket!

But being a committed responsible parent doesn't mean being selfless at any cost. Being self-less can at times be harmful, particularly when it means we deny our "selves" in the relationship.

My "self" is my inner being. Without this "self" I am valueless. The "self" is what makes each one of us unique and special. This "self" is what we bring to our parenthood.

It's important, therefore, to respect and develop our "selves" while we enrich, respect, develop, and appreciate the "selves" of our children.

How can we expect our children to respect us if we ourselves don't respect our "selves", if we don't show "self"-respect? If we want our children to have "self"-esteem, we must build and develop ours first, focusing on our strengths, valuing our achievements, and acknowledging our uniqueness.

Parents who continually enrich their "selves" teach their children the value of "self"-care. They don't feel that they lost out in life or that someone owed them for it. They don't blame their children for unfulfilled hopes. They have no need to find excuses or scapegoats because they experience inner-emptiness.

They don't waste or sacrifice their lives because of their children.

They don't derive a sense of importance from being "sacrificing martyr-parents."

As role models they are responsible for their "selves," and they therefore bring up children who enrich their lives rather than rob them of it.

They value the "selves" of their children and do not hurt them by making them victims or by demanding from them a lifetime payback.

They know and understand that their children make their lives whole.

We damage our children's "self"-esteem when we show their "selves" no respect. Children think that the way we treat them is the way they deserve to be treated. When we respect them, they feel their "self"-worth. It proves that we accept, care for, and value them, and it helps them develop their own "self"-respect and "self"-esteem.

As a mother-parent, I must be a role model for all aspects of my children's lives while they are under my wings and for later, when they fly from the nest and start their own families. So, the way I bring up my children affects my grandchildren, too.

BOTTOM LINE:

As role models we respect our "selves" and value the 'selves' of our children.

4.

HAVING CHILDREN IS CREATIVE AND JOYFUL

I become upset when I hear parents describe parenthood as "hard work" or "hard labor" — criminals get sentenced to hard labor! If that's our attitude, we ruin things from the start.

What do we expect children to feel and learn when they hear their parents using descriptions like this?

We decided to become parents. It wasn't a punishment or a court sentence. And as to what should come first, our marriage or our children? The answer is neither. There is no competition between our marriage and our children. Neither should be the loser! We are all winners.

Are our marriage and our children two separate entities or two fighting camps, each striving for victory?

Marriage and children are complementary parts of the whole that is the family! We should be attentive to our personal needs, our needs as a married couple, and the individual needs of each of our children.

Children who participate and share their lives with their parents feel part of the family and enrich the marriage. They don't have to misbehave and cause problems in order to be noticed and included, because they know that their place in the family is secure.

Motherhood consists of many components, among which are love, respect, appreciation, trust, empathy, guidance, thoughtfulness, commitment, and a great deal of joy. Motherhood is a serious matter — it's not funny, but it's great fun!

Parenthood is the most creative and enriching process in our lives. I have been quite creative in my personal life. I have painted, drawn, sculpted, taught, and written a book of short stories. None of these can even begin to match the creativity of my motherhood. Without my girls, my life would have been lacking, no matter what I achieved or attained otherwise.

BOTTOM LINE:

Instead of using negative language when talking about bringing up our children, let's rather focus on the joy this creativity brings to our marriage and our lives.

5.

OUR DREAMS BELONG TO US AND OUR CHILDREN'S DREAMS BELONG TO THEM

Our children were born to have and fulfill their own dreams, not *our* dreams. Although our children are our creations, *they don't belong to us in any way.* They have their own unique "selves," ambitions, needs, and dreams.

If, for instance, I once had the unrealized dream of becoming a dancer, I have no right to impose my dream on my daughter who wishes to become a school teacher.

I know a man who became a dentist because that was what his father wanted him to be. His own dream was to be a lawyer or a musician. Guess what? He now has two sons — one is a lawyer and one a musician!

We are here to fulfill our own dreams, not those of our parents. Our children are here to fulfill *their* dreams.

Imposing our dreams and ambitions on our children stops them from developing the way they choose. It doesn't allow them to be what they wish to be.

Kahlil Gibran, in *The Prophet,* says the following about parents and children:

"You are the bows from which your children as living arrows are sent forth."

They come from us, but they are not us. By encouraging and supporting their pursuit of their own dreams and goals, we free them to be what they have the right to become.

We are presumptuous if we expect our children to achieve what we failed to achieve. And it's improper to seek our fulfillment through their success.

What if they resist our demands?

And what if they fail?

Do we love them less?

Do we attach conditions to our love for the children we decided to have?

If we want happy and successful children, we must allow them to chase their own dreams. Their lives belong to them — it's not our second chance at living!

I did not reward my daughters by giving them money or presents for their achievements in school, sports, art, or other activities.

A reward is a manipulative and controlling tool used by the person with power. In a sense, it is used the same way as punishment.

It teaches children that they have to perform, act, or behave in certain ways in order to win our approval and attention. It encourages them to live in order to please those who have power over them. It teaches them to fulfill the demands and dreams of others and, in the process, to deny their own needs, goals, and dreams.

Rewarding is conditioning and controlling. It shackles rather than frees.

My daughters did not fulfill my dreams and didn't achieve for me. I encouraged and supported them. The success was theirs. I shared their joy.

BOTTOM LINE:

Let's allow and encourage our children to dream and chase their own rainbows.

6.
WHY SHOULD MY CHILD BE LIKE SOMEONE ELSE?

Children shouldn't live our lives for us, nor should they be expected to behave and act like other family members. We should never compare one child to another within the family or to any other kids we know.

When we ask a child, "What's the matter with you? Why can't you do well at school like your sister?" (or "like your cousin?" or "like your friend John?"), we declare the child a failure and invite her or him to resent the other child, the "successful" one.

Why should any child, who is a unique person, be *like* someone else?

And if for some reason, our children do want to be like someone else, let them find their own models and not force our choices on them. They have the right to choose for themselves! Nor should we compare our children to ourselves.

What is a mother trying to accomplish when she says to her daughter something like, "What's wrong with you? At your age I was so successful with boys," or "At your age I did so well at school, and look at you?" What is the child's answer supposed to be? How is the child supposed to feel after such a put-down? It's unfair competition!

Do we have children in order to compete with or win against them? Would we, as parents, like to be compared to others and be made to feel inadequate?

Did we like it when our parents did this to us and made us feel like failures? For that matter, how often do we hear parents stating that one child is "the clever one" like his or her father and the second child is "the pretty one" like his or her mother?

Why make comparisons? And what happens when we have a child who isn't "clever" or "pretty"? To which of the parents will he or she be compared? Each child is special and different and should be respected accordingly.

BOTTOM LINE:

Treat our children as unique individuals without comparing them to others.

7.
LET'S TRY EMPATHY

The day before my older daughter, Orit, started school, I wrote down what I thought her feelings must have been. Many years later I found those lines and showed them to her for the first time.

Here they are:

I have waited for this moment for a long time. Tomorrow I start first grade — a big day for me — the biggest in my life. What will really happen tomorrow?

Mom is very excited, although she's trying to hide it so that she doesn't make me too jumpy. And I am so happy. I have heard so much about school from the older children in our street. Some of the stories are nice, but others are scary. So, I'm also a bit confused and frightened.

Mom has bought me all the things I need, so I'm organized and ready to start school. But, as I said before, I'm confused.

There are so many things I don't know. There are so many questions without answers:

Who will my teacher be?

Will he or she like me?

Who else will be in my class?

Will I make friends easily?

All this is so important to me.

At the dinner table I try my best to behave. But every now and then my excitement becomes unbearable and I burst out with my questions, disturbing everyone else's conversation.

Mom answers my questions patiently. She wants to know if I'm happy to be starting school tomorrow. Oh Mom, how can I express everything that is boiling inside me? Of course I'm happy, but everything is new and strange. Will I really be able to handle it?

After supper I can't settle down. I'm so restless, and I don't know what to do with myself. Mom and Dad let me stay up later tonight. They say that now I'm starting school, I'm sort of grown-up, so it's okay to sleep a bit less at night — as if I could sleep anyway!

Now it's really late. I've been in bed for a long time, but I can't fall asleep. The house is quiet; it's very dark outside; but there is no sleep for me. When I can't handle things any longer, I go to my parent's room. I wish I could sleep peacefully like them. They seem so strong and sure of themselves. I finally fall asleep on my comforter next to their bed.

I wake up very early, get dressed, and wait for Mom to take me to school. I can't eat, can't even think of it. All I want is to be there. Suddenly, in the car on the way to school, I know that I'll be fine. Somehow, I know that I'll make it. I'm not alone, am I?

When we arrive at the school, I hold Mom's hand and together we walk through the gate, the entrance to my new world.

***

Empathy is one of the most important ingredients of motherhood, parenthood, and any human relationships that we create.

Whenever any of my daughters asked me for something and my immediate intention was to say "no," I would take my time before giving an answer.

I would listen to her reasons for the request and put myself in her shoes. I would ask myself, "Has she the right to have what she is asking for? If I were in her place, what would I have expected from my mother?" I try to empathize and be fair.

Even if my answer was negative, I made sure my child understood why. Whatever my dealings with them, I tried to put myself in their shoes and make sure I was fair.

The girls understood from an early age that they couldn't play one parent against the other. If I said "no," they would not get a "yes" from their father, or vice-versa, because Terry and I discussed their needs and requests and agreed on our decisions.

Even though Terry didn't spend as much time with them as I did and many of the on-the-spot decisions were mine, we always discussed them later.

BOTTOM LINE:

Both parents must consider a child's requests with respect and empathy, regardless of how mundane the requests might be.
To avoid and prevent conflicts, we should always ask ourselves the following:
— If I were a child now, would I want to be treated this way?
— When I was a child, was I happy when my parents treated me in this manner?
How did I want to be treated?

8.
SEEING OUR DECISIONS THROUGH WILL HELP AVOID FUTURE CONFLICTS

We listen to a child's request, discuss it with the child, think about it, and come up with a decision. If we say "yes," we should honor that promise to the child and not change our mind later. If we say "no," we should stay with it even if we get pressured by the child.

We should be prepared to be flexible, but if we routinely let the child change our decisions because we want to be "nice," we create an invitation to repeated conflicts in the future.

If we want to be "nice," we should say "yes" to start with. Once we have decided, we stick with our decision. We need to be consistent.

My friends' son is twelve years old. He has many friends with whom he socializes, mainly during the weekend. I was visiting them one Friday evening and heard him ask his parents what time he should return home from a party.

The parents told him to be back, inside the house, at eleven o'clock sharp. He agreed.

At exactly eleven that night, the phone rang. It was the boy, asking his parents if he could stay at the party an hour longer. The parents argued with him and brought it down to half an hour.

During this discussion, the parents forgot that the time when their son phoned was actually the time when he was supposed to be at home!

The kid was smart and knew his parents so well that instead of saying he was sorry for not being home as agreed, he hijacked the conversation in another direction by negotiating with them on the extra time.

If he had found the party exciting and wanted to stay longer — this happens, and we can allow ourselves to be flexible at times — he should have phoned earlier, not at the hour when he was supposed to be at home!

What is the value of my decision if I don't follow it through? What message am I sending to my child about myself?

What does the child learn from me about adult behavior?

Within the family, parents create and enforce guidelines, boundaries, and rules for the children.

Children need freedom to think and develop, but that doesn't mean *total* freedom.

As long as we live within the framework of society, none of us has total freedom. We are all bound by laws and codes of behavior. And so are our children. They need to know and understand the rules of their family. As they grow older, they should be allowed to have their own input into the rules and to participate in creating them.

These rules should make sense and be fair. Rules that are too rigid punish the child and the parents alike and threaten to make the child rebellious or fearful.

On the other hand, complete freedom for children, without structure or guidelines, leads to chaos, confusion, and uncertainty.

Limits teach children how to live in the world, those behaviors that work and those that don't.

Too many possibilities and choices can paralyze them. If we say or imply that they can do whatever they wish, they may feel incapable of deciding or choosing; they may feel inadequate. Although it's normal and natural for our children to keep testing our rules and decisions, deep down they want and need the structure of constructive boundaries to make them feel safe.

If our children test us to see how far they can go and if we are not strong enough to enforce the limits, we enter into an ongoing game of power and control between us (the parents) and them (the kids). This division within the family serves no constructive purpose.

We are all part of the family, a whole entity, not a collection of battling factions. We must merge firmness and fairness, love and discipline, and consistently enforce our rules and decisions with dignity and respect.

Once, our cat disappeared. Orit and Tal asked me to replace it with a new one. I explained why I was against the idea, and for a while there was no mention of the subject.

One day after work, as I entered the house and greeted the girls, I sensed something was different. I ate lunch with them, all the while aware that something was in the air.

Then there was a sound — a "meow"— and I knew. I looked at the girls, waiting for an explanation.

"My friend Joy had new kittens," Orit volunteered at last. "She asked me if I wanted one, so I got us a kitten."

"I know you want a cat. We spoke about it many times, and I told you that the answer was 'no' and it's still 'no'," I explained. I didn't shout at her. I wasn't upset or angry. In fact, I was amused and impressed with her determination. But I wasn't going to have a new cat in the house!

"So what can I do now?" she asked me. "I can't return the kitten. I already took it!"

"That's your problem and responsibility, not mine. You got yourself into this situation, now you have to handle it all on you own."

"Joy lives so far! How can I carry the cat to her?" she asked.

"I'll tell you what. I'll drive you and the kitten to Joy and spare you the walk. But you'll go in, apologize, and explain that you can't have the kitten," I said.

"What reason can I give for returning the kitten?" she asked. "Just tell her the truth," I suggested.

I drove her and the kitten to Joy and waited outside, in the car, while she returned the cat. She seemed very relieved when she returned. "What did you tell Joy?" I asked.

"I apologized and explained that, against your wishes and without your knowing about it, I took the kitten, and that it was wrong and therefore I couldn't keep it." And that was the end of the incident.

BOTTOM LINE:

Stick with our decisions and follow through with them.

9.
KEEP AND RESPECT OUR CHILDREN'S COMMITMENTS

If we want to bring up responsible children, we need to teach and show them what responsibility is.

Say they are supposed to be at a certain place at a certain time in order to participate in some activity. No matter how young they are, we must make sure that they are ready and present on time. This is our responsibility.

Children need to be honored and respected, and their commitments must be regarded as important as ours. We may need to plan ahead in order to avoid upsetting or embarrassing them.

If children are always late, other children notice it. Chances are that these children never learn to plan and organize their own time. Later in life, this can affect their ability to meet deadlines or cause them to be viewed as irresponsible.

Once, many years ago, I visited a friend for tea. She had invited the girls and me for three in the afternoon on a certain Saturday.

We looked forward to that day and planned accordingly, making sure we arrived on time.

After welcoming us, my friend apologized, saying she had to take her children to a birthday party that had started at two o'clock and for which they were already late.

"Would you mind waiting here for me?" she casually asked. I was mad! Because I worked during the week, I planned my weekend time carefully.

The main reason my girls had joined me was to play with my friend's kids and now they were off to a party! We made all the effort in the world to keep this appointment and what did we achieve?

What was I supposed to say?

I could have said that we made an effort to be on time and that we did not expect to be left waiting for at least half an hour, the time it would take her to drive to the party and back.

I could have said that she should have phoned to say she was running late and ask if we could come a little later.

I could have asked why she invited my kids when hers were going to a party.

I could have said that she let us all down, including her own children, for whom she caused the anxiety of arriving an hour late at the party.

But I did none of these. It wasn't the right time or the right place. So the girls and I waited for her return.

She returned with two upset children, one of them in tears.

"What happened?" I asked. "Why are they not at the party?" "Oh, it's nothing serious. I made a mistake. The party was last week. I didn't check my diary. They'll get over it," she said casually.

If we lived completely alone, our time would be ours and whatever we did or didn't do wouldn't affect or upset anyone else.

However, when we live within a family, work, or social group and fail to keep our agreements, we affect others adversely.

At times things do happen and we are forced to change some commitments. But it mustn't be on a regular basis and certainly not at the expense of our kids or others who do keep their word.

BOTTOM LINE:

We are responsible for bringing up responsible children.

10.
NO SPOILED BRATS

Our children need to know that every day is not "child's day."

We don't want to raise spoiled brats who think that life is only about them and what their parents should do for them.

Many of us are obsessed with our children's happiness. We want them to always feel good. This is an impossible, unrealistic, and unhealthy goal. We become doormats for them.

In order to shelter our kids from unhappiness, some of us do whatever we think it takes to protect them from disappointments.

Instead of allowing them to live and learn from their disappointments and mistakes, we enslave ourselves to our children and their desires.

Then we complain about "this generation of spoiled brats," who of course are being raised by other parents and never by us!

We end up with spoiled and irresponsible children, and we only have ourselves to blame.

As part of a family, we naturally share the duties and chores at home. Children should be given tasks appropriate for their age.

They should see to their rooms, clean, feed the pets, help in the garden, help in the kitchen, wash the car, etc. These chores should not be for money; children contribute as their abilities allow for the good of the family, just as their parents do.

Most kids enjoy helping their parents; it makes them feel grown-up and mature. If we encourage them and show appreciation instead of criticizing, we will get their cooperation.

We also need to be careful not to shower our children with material things. Many parents think that buying presents for their children shows proof of their love. It doesn't.

Children feel loved because of the way they are treated, not because of the presents they receive. Parents who can't afford to buy gifts love their children no less than those who buy them everything. Presents and material things are no substitutes for love!

Children should get what we think they need according to our means and their age, not according to what other kids have or what they see on television.

They shouldn't order us or dictate their demands to us. They need to know there are limits. Children who get everything they want grow up appreciating nothing and expecting everything from others, as if it's their right to always get whatever they want. Again, if our children turn out that way, it's not their fault. It's ours.

BOTTOM LINE:

Spoiled brats are created by their parents.

11.
THE IMPORTANCE OF MUTUAL TRUST

I remember a father who very proudly told me how he taught his son about trust.

When the boy was about four years old, the father put him on a high chair and told him to jump. The boy didn't jump, because he was scared. "Don't worry. Nothing will happen to you. I'll catch you," the father reassured him.

So the child jumped, fell on the floor, hurt himself, and cried. "You see," the father triumphantly told me, "I didn't catch my boy, and so I gave him the best lesson a father can give his child. I wanted him to learn to never trust anyone, not even his own father!" he said, grinning with great satisfaction.

I was stunned and speechless.

What this father did was criminal! If this child couldn't trust his own father and the rest of the world at that young age, how was he ever supposed to find safety?

This boy's father robbed him of the right to feel secure and safe and made him suspicious of the whole world. And after his own father lied to him, why shouldn't this child from that day on lie to his parents and the world?

I felt desperately sorry for the boy.

What this man expressed was totally opposite to what I stand for.

I believe in bringing up honest and trustworthy children who will grow up to be honest and trustworthy adults.

When our children tell us that they keep good company, avoid drugs, do their schoolwork, drive our car only with our permission, whatever they tell us... we should be able to trust them.

In order to achieve this trust, we have to set the example. We should keep our word and our promises and not tell lies.

We have to be honest and straight with our children. If we aren't trustworthy ourselves, we have no right to expect or demand it from them. That would be hypocrisy.

BOTTOM LINE:

We create mutual trust between our children and ourselves by modeling it ourselves.

12.
THE QUESTION OF PUNISHMENT

"To punish or not to punish? This is the question."

Punishment, by definition, means causing somebody else to feel pain physically, emotionally, or mentally.

Punishment is manipulative. It is based on external control exercised by someone who has power.

What's the purpose of punishment and why does a child get punished?

We mustn't punish a child in order to hurt him or her. If we have to punish, our purpose must be to *educate and teach*. We want to train the child to be self-motivated, not to react to us out of fear.

At times a child may do something wrong because we create confusion by not being clear about what is allowed. At other times the child may misbehave in order to get attention. Sometimes, feelings expressed as negative behavior are cries for our assistance.

When bad behavior repeats itself, it is important to take notice and find out what the problem really is.

As a teacher and a mother, I recognize that children are always learning and that making mistakes is part of the process.

We won't need to punish our children if we adhere to the following principles:

— Communicate with children;

— Honor and trust them;

— Respect them;

— Make sure that boundaries and rules are clearly stated and explained;

— Insist that the rules be respected;

— Explain that there are consequences for violating the family rules;

— Consistently enforce the rules.

If a child knowingly does something wrong or knowingly keeps on doing the wrong things, as long as we are sure there isn't any serious underlying problem, it is important to deal with the unacceptable behavior. A child needs to be taught that there are consequences to behavior and that bad behavior is not acceptable.

In order to give value to punishment and prevent more of the same behavior in the future, punishment should be followed by clear and positive communication. Children must understand what happened and learn that they are responsible for their actions and the consequences. Children need to know that we value them but that some behavior is unacceptable.

Any punishment we impose should be proportionate to the misbehavior; if a child leaves his or her shoes in the wrong place, he or she should not be grounded for a month!

Once we have told children that we intend to punish them, we should be consistent, follow through with our decision, and see that the punishment is carried out, just as we enforce anything else we state as a rule or a decision.

Punishing children by hitting them is physical abuse. Sometimes, after other forms of punishment have failed to achieve their goal, especially when the child's safety is at risk, a child might deserve a spanking (which should be given only with the hand and only on the rear).

Our response should be to educate, not to hurt. Pulling, twisting, or pinching parts of the body are inappropriate and abusive.

Most parents spank for two main reasons: to change a child's behavior and to let out their own anger and frustration. The combination of power and anger seldom encourages the child to improve. On the contrary, it creates resentment.

The more we punish, the less value the punishment has. It's like school, where teachers who shout and punish regularly lose their power. Students treat it like a game and learn nothing positive from it. It becomes a joke!

We don't want to be a joke, nor would we like to represent a joke!

Our goal must not be to control, but to help our children develop the ability to think, judge, make their own decisions and become self-disciplined and responsible.

BOTTOM LINE:

Punishment is a serious statement that should educate our children, not hurt or damage them.

13.
PARENTS AND TEACHERS

Some parents view schools as the main source of instruction and discipline for their kids.

From the time their children enter school, these parents enter a form of retirement; they relinquish their responsibility for their child's well being. Without anyone's actually discussing the issue with them, teachers become the ones responsible.

When things are okay with the child, these parents claim that all is well — thanks to them, of course.

But:

— If the child is not disciplined, it is the school's fault;

— If the child is not doing well, it's the school's fault;

— If the child is noisy, non-communicative, on drugs, sexually active at the age of twelve, irresponsible, disrespectful, etc., it's because of the school!

How convenient it is for these "retired" parents to blame others! What an easy way out it is for parents who are not really interested in their kids! They are too busy "living their own lives," "doing their own thing," and "finding themselves."

They might "find themselves" while losing their children in the process.

People who understand why they have children and affirm their commitments to their kids also know what their responsibilities are. They recognize that they cannot "do their own thing" and "live their own lives" at the expense of their children.

Most of the time our children spend learning *skills* is spent in school, but we parents, are their most important teachers. Ideally parents and teachers should combine efforts and work together for the benefit of the children; they are not two distinct camps.

As parents, we must never forget that the child is ours, that we, not the school, brought him or her into the world.

During their school years, our children have many teachers. Each teacher has a commitment to his or her pupils during the time he or she teaches them. But by the nature of the occupation, teachers come and go. Parents are there to stay!

While there are part-time teachers, there cannot and must not be a part-time parent!

I often watch television talk shows, documentaries, and movies dealing with troubled kids. It does not cease to amaze me how many parents from all walks of life, regardless of their education or financial situation, are not there for their kids. They are "parents in absentia."

Some disappear completely from the scene. Others are there physically, but only as "retired" or "part-time" parents.

These parents may say that, because of others, they "cannot cope." They take the easiest line of resistance, blaming the Internet, the media, and the schools for their children's problems. The whole world is at fault. These parents seldom admit that they are the reason why their children turned out the way they did.

This reminds me of a syphilis epidemic in Conyers, Georgia, among upper and middle class, multi-racial school kids between twelve and eighteen years old.

Most of these kids lived in big homes where each family member could disappear into his or her own room equipped with television, computer, and phone. They lived with parents who both worked in order to achieve this expensive life style.

The kids were left at home unsupervised. The parents had no clues about what they were doing. A group of these "free" children became very active sexually, even using their parents' homes for their sexual encounters while the parents were at work or out of town. Some of these kids had between twenty and a hundred partners during this time period.

These parents who didn't communicate or connect with their children and focused only on their own lives, were "parents in absentia" — they really weren't there.

When the kids got sick, they blamed the whole world

for their children's bizarre and way-out sexual activities. It was every one's fault but theirs.

After all was said, the question still remained as to *whose children were they anyway?*

Recently I met a university student who told me that she feels privileged and grateful to have such a great family as hers.

She said that in the past, she had taken her parents for-granted and hadn't appreciated them. But after she left home, the stories other students told about their families made her realize how lucky she really had been.

In order to fit in, she would also tell stories, complaining about her parents. Other students would just laugh at her. She then tried to be creative by fabricating stories. They still laughed at her. Now she doesn't even try.

"What can I say when I hear them talk about parents who drink, parents who disappear, or parents who are abusive?" she asked me. "I come from a loving and caring family with parents who are always there for me. What a shame that I had to realize my parents' value through hearing all these terrible stories. And what a shame that instead of my family being the norm, it often is not. I really am very lucky."

BOTTOMLINE:

We must always be there for our kids and take full responsibility for the outcome.

Dear Mommy

Thank you for being such
a wonderful mother

I love you

Dear Mom

Please get better soon.

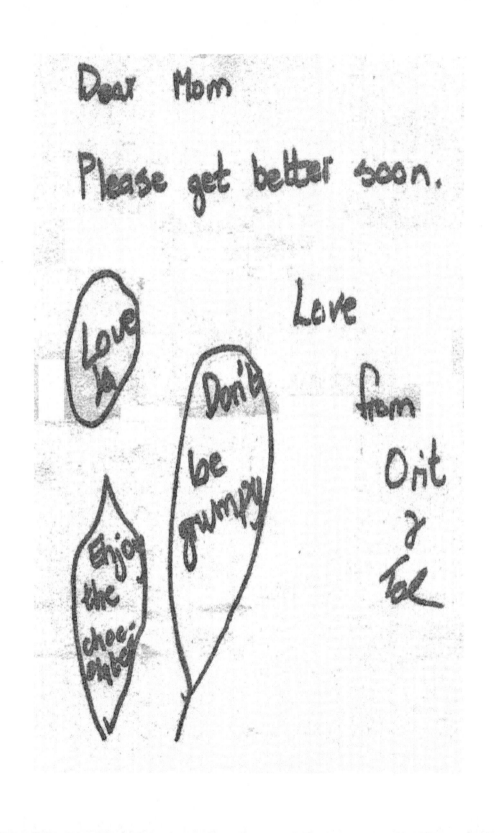

Love

Love
is

Don't
be
grumpy

from

Enjoy
the
choc-
olates

Orit
&
Tal

Dear Mom

Thank-you for the beautiful

shoes and takkies you bought

me this morning. And thanks

for being so kind and patient.

Love

from

Ritca

Dear Mommy Noya

Thank-you for being

loving, kind and under-

standing. Sorry for my
naughty behaviour yesterday

I absolutely

love and adore
you. You're

the greatest mum

in the WORLD!
thats SUPERMUM

Thank You

To the best mother in the whole world. I sincerely say THANK-YOU for being so nice to me when I came home in tears this avi(afternoon)

You and daddy are really wonderful, outstanding, loving and caring people.

Lots

of

Love

Riti,
Ritca,
Pritca,
Rit-root
and
Orit.

Thank You

To the best mother
in the whole world.

I sincerely say
THANK - YOU for being
so nice to me when I came
home in tears this avi(afternoon)

You and daddy are really
wonderful, outstanding, loving
and caring people,

Lots

of

Love

Riti,
Ritca,
Pnkca
Rit-root
and
Orit.

Dear Mommy

Thank-you very much for being
so caring for the past few days,
I don't think that I could've managed
to make it without you! I really love you
and care for you very much, there is nothing
in the entire world that I wouldn't do
for you!

I Love you
very much!

Love
Tali
~x~

Dear Mammale

We love you!

Your

Gooties

Orti and Shnoofy

when ya gonna turn
over a **NEW LEAF**....
... and write?

Dear Mommy

I am very sorry
what I did please
~~forgive~~ forgive me
for being irritable

Love

from

Tali

Dear Mommy

I love you so much!

P.S. Please don't leave me
at home again!

14.
GRANDPARENTHOOD IS
NOT A SECOND CHANCE

With each child, we have only one chance at being a mother and a parent.

When our child becomes a parent and we become grandparents, it is not a second chance for us to be parents. Our role then is to be only grandparents-supportive, caring, and loving. We can't interfere, nor should we assume the responsibility of a parent.

We had our chance!

We need to let go and allow our children to be responsible for their own lives. There are, of course, extreme cases, such as when a child loses his or her parents, and the grandparents take over. But these are not normal circumstances.

At times it may be tempting to take charge, particularly when we feel guilty for messing up as parents. Our problem is our guilt. Interfering can create even more problems between us and the kids we feel guilty about.

Our children need to fulfill their own dreams and live their own lives. Being parents is an important part of that.

When our children become parents, they have to deal not only with us, but with their parents-in-law, too. Four grandparents are involved, which means four different egos to deal with!

Whenever we feel the need to take over, we should ask ourselves, "How did I feel when my parents did that to me?" or "How did it feel when my parents-in law interfered with the way I brought up my children?"

We should be able to communicate with our kids about matters concerning their children, but the decisions are theirs, not ours. We had our chance at parenting.

Just as we must respect our children and their own roles as parents, they must respect us as grandparents, not as parents!

They should not take us, the grandparents, for-granted, nor should they demand or impose parental responsibility on us whenever they feel like it.

Once they decide to have children, it becomes their chance at parenting. The responsibility is theirs, not their parents'.

It isn't right when children play upon their parents' guilt. When asked, grandparents should only do what they feel is appropriate for them to do and feel free to say "no" when "no" is the appropriate answer. Grandparents must avoid participating in an on-going manipulative game.

I cringe when I hear grandparents saying, in front of their own kids, that for them it's much nicer to be a grandparent than of being a parent — as if there is any comparison.

What a shame they feel that way! What a waste of the opportunity they had to experience the greatest role of their lives.

They are comparing two completely different roles, that of a full-time, life-long, totally committed, responsible parent and that of a come-and-go, fun-loving, and supportive grandparent. One is totally involved while the other is thoroughly voluntary.

Some go even further and say that they love their grandchildren more than their own children. How are their children supposed to feel on hearing this? Would these grandparents have liked to hear their own parents say that?

There is no need to make these comparisons; each role has its unique value. Nor is there any need to compare how we felt about our kids and how we feel about our grandchildren. Each of them is unique, and our feelings toward them are different. And even if we do think that we love one more than the other, we should keep our thoughts to ourselves. There is no need to embarrass and upset anyone.

BOTTOM LINE:

Out of respect, our parents do not take away our responsibility to our children. Out of respect, we do not impose our parental responsibility on our parents.

15.
MORE OF MY OWN PERSONAL "DO'S" AND "DON'TS"

I wanted my daughters to have self-esteem, values, independence and balance. I wanted them to be responsible, communicative, confident, and happy.

Here are more of the things I did in the hope of achieving this goal:

A. Enriching my life

When I became a mother, I gave up work. Although it was difficult for us financially, I felt that it was important for me to be with our children from the start.

I did carry on developing my "self," however. I completed a Master's degree at a university, even though I had to take out a loan to do it.

There are some additional, important aspects of enriching the "self."

Because many children spend more time with their mothers, the mother often takes responsibility for the children's health, education, discipline, emotional and physical well-being, and so on. She often has to act as teacher, cook, physician, coach, cleaning lady, driver, psychologist, dietitian, etc.

To be able to cope, she must have some time for herself out of the house and away from the children.

Some mothers think that they need to sacrifice their own welfare for their child's sake. By doing this, they lose balance.

A mother must attend to her own needs and not fall into the trap of self-neglect. Sacrifices undermine her well-being and keep her from performing at her best. She becomes a less effective mother.

After the initial period of becoming a mother and getting used to the newcomer, a woman should make sure that her "self" isn't neglected and that she isn't obsessed with her maternal role twenty-four hours a day.

She must continuously enrich her "self." If she doesn't look after her "self" she might eventually resent having had children!

There is nothing more boring than a woman who can talk only about her children. A drained, bored, boring, and unhappy woman cannot enrich her children's lives. She doesn't contribute much to her marriage, either!

The birth of a child does not mean the death of the mother's "self."

Even if she doesn't work, a mother can read, study, have a hobby, meet with friends without children, go to lectures, attend concerts, etc.

She mustn't forget and neglect her physical- "self." Instead, she should continue to exercise, eat correctly, and watch her appearance.

Going out with her husband alone is very important. As much as parents need to spend time with their children, they also need to be together without them.

She shouldn't focus only on her children — she needs variation in order to charge her battery.

BOTTOM LINE:

Becoming a mother is no reason for self-neglect.

B. I didn't do the schoolwork for my children

At some point, I had to admit to myself and to my inquisitive daughters that I didn't know all the answers to all subjects. No one actually knows everything about everything, but we do have the key and the access to the answers.

Instead of doing their work and finding the answers for them, I showed them how to find it by themselves. I taught them how to use the dictionary, the atlas, the encyclopedia, bibliographies, etc.

After they started school, I assisted them with the schoolwork. I also checked their schoolwork, making sure it was done correctly and on time.

I showed a great deal of interest in what they did and encouraged them. When they did well I shared their happiness. With time they didn't need me at all!

They handled every project, exam, and thesis by themselves. They learned to trust and respect themselves and felt proud of their ability, independence, and maturity.

The more parents and teachers allow children to do for themselves at school and at home, the more they learn that we believe in them.

BOTTOM LINE:

We don't fish for the kids; we teach them how to fish.

C. Entertaining wasn't my responsibility

A mother isn't a perpetual entertainment unit!

At an early age, the girls knew that I didn't want to hear the sentence, "Mom, I am bored. There's nothing to do." I made sure they had enough creative and stimulating things at home to keep them busy.

They drew, painted, read, listened to music, created their own dances, put on shows, played with toys and games, played with creative games, and, of course, played with other kids. They were very busy, to say the least — so busy, in fact, that they typically went to sleep at seven thirty in the evening. Would anyone believe me if I said that I used to beg them to stay up a bit longer?

I introduced them to classical music and concerts, to ballet, theater, and the worlds of art and science. We went to galleries and museums.

I told them that they should never feel alone. Wherever they are in the world, they have "friends" they can visit — concerts, movies, theater shows, art exhibitions etc.

Although I did a lot with my kids when they were young, they didn't depend on me to provide entertainment for them. They learned to keep themselves busy and to be self-sufficient.

BOTTOM LINE:

The word "boredom" doesn't appear in our vocabulary.

D. My daughters were always part of the family

I included the girls in as many activities as I could — knowing that they belonged, made them feel important.

From an early age they ate with us, no matter what the place looked like after the meal.

We spent most of our vacations together. Terry and I got great pleasure from being able to share everything with them.

Every year I celebrated my birthday twice, once with my husband and daughters and once again with my extended family, my girlfriends. I would either have my friends over for a bite at home or take them out for a brunch or lunch. And of course, my two friends, Orit and Tal, took part in the event.

One time, a friend of ours, an engineer, told us how upset he was with his kids. He had asked his children, ages twenty and seventeen, to describe his role in the family. All they could come up with was that he was the one who made salads in the evenings.

They weren't joking. Nor was he!

There is nothing wrong with his salad contribution every evening — it's creative and healthy. I do think however, that it was his own fault they didn't have more to say about him.

I made sure that Tal and Orit knew where their

parents worked and what we did. They visited our workplaces on occasions and met our colleagues.

When they were very young, it wasn't that easy to explain what I did. When I received my PhD in literature, I told them, "I am now a doctor."

They excitedly said that this was great because they would not have to go to the family doctor any longer.

I tried hard to explain the abstract concept of a university degree in literature, to girls of six and five. Eventually I gave up my complicated explanations and said that I wasn't a doctor for people, only for books and stories.

They were always joyous and active participants in our lives.

BOTTOM LINE:

Our children are part of the family and should be made to feel that way.

E. No mocking or labeling

As a teacher at a high school and a lecturer at university, I made a vow to myself never to hurt any of my students with upsetting remarks. I was there to build them, not to destroy them.

There is a lot in common between parents and the teachers into whose hands we thrust the future, our children.

It is easy for an adult to diminish a child by mocking and belittling. We need to be careful with the manner in which we use our tongue. It can be a dangerous weapon, capable of wounding and even killing.

When we deal with young people, our responsibility is not to hurt or insult them in public or at home.

There is no need to be sarcastic or humiliating with a child, even on those occasions when we aren't happy with the child. When we use cutting remarks, we abuse. It's as bad as hitting the child, and at times it's even more painful.

Resorting to a destructive usage of our tongue with our kids is a sign of our own shortcomings. It means that we failed.

Labeling a child is another dangerous way in which we use our tongue. Even when it is "positive," it is still labeling. What do we expect of children if we tell them that they are stupid, ugly, fat, clumsy, uncreative, unintelligent, horrible, ungrateful, etc.?

Once we categorized them, put them in a box, or gave them a negative title, we are finished. Why should they even try to behave differently if we have already made up our minds about them?

They will live up or down to our expectations. Even the smart ones will keep on acting like idiots or fools and do badly at school.

Even if a child *is* slow and battles at school, we still have no right to call that child stupid. How smart are *we* if that's the way we handle the problem?

We are the stupid ones. If we were bright, we wouldn't address the child in this manner. And even if a child *is* ugly, is that his or her fault?

Are we all so beautiful, and does it really matter? Maybe we should take another look at our own reflections in the mirror before using our tongues!

Some of us are convinced that no child of ours could be merely normal or just average. We make it a matter of ego to produce and create a specially gifted and perfect child. In reality, no child is perfect and every child is special.

If we give one child in the family a positive label such as gifted, genius, beautiful, talented, or clever, and say nothing comparable about our other kids, how are these other children supposed to feel?

If we declare one special, what does that make the others?

By elevating one child, do we invite the others to feel inadequate, dumb, or hostile? And how is the "gifted" child supposed to feel if we or the school praise him or her at the expense of the other kids in the family or at school?

We shouldn't be surprised if this child walks around like a peacock, thinking that even parents and teachers are inferior because not even they wear the crown of the gifted.

Do we really want to give a child the license to separate herself or himself from others and become alienated? Isn't it more important at times to us than to the child to have the child declared gifted, because it reflects well on us and does our ego good?

And how many of us with low self-esteem hope to feel worthy because we produced a "gifted" child?

When we wish for perfection, we impose our high expectations on our child. We become controlling and manipulative.

What if the child cannot deliver? How will he or she feel? Do we want him or her to feel like a failure?

How do you suppose a "gifted" child feels when we demand things of him or her and leave other siblings alone? Does this seem fair to the child? Will he or she resent us and the other siblings?

There are many definitions of giftedness. Even among the gifted there are differences. Highly gifted children differ from the moderately gifted ones as much as the latter differ from average children. What exactly does "gifted" mean, when the same person can be gifted in one area and a thorough misfit in others?

Soon after Orit started elementary school, the school suggested to us that she participate in a program for gifted children. After Terry and I attended some lectures to understand what that meant, we decided against it.

As much as it would have been a compliment to the child, we felt that if we labeled her "gifted," she might have to pay the price of ending up alienated and separated.

It is okay for each of us to deal differently with the individual concerns of our own children. For many parents, the option of having their children participate in programs for gifted children is important. Many kids do participate in them. Nevertheless, it is also important to be aware of the price a child might pay for wearing this desired label.

As long as there is balance in our children's lives, as long as they are cared for emotionally, intellectually, physically, and socially, and as long as they are involved, occupied, interested, and have fun at school and at home, they'll do just fine.

They need to grow whole and rounded. Focusing on one aspect while neglecting the others can be costly for the child.

Home and the school together should create a nurturing environment that fosters the gifts our children have. People are all different; in the real world we need to know how to live, work, and socialize with one another, not to set ourselves apart from each other.

More and more we hear about the importance of emotional intelligence. It means our ability to handle ourselves and each other as individuals and as parts of a family, a team, or a group. At times, our social skills and abilities are more important than our education and intelligence.

Consider the parents who want their child to graduate from an Ivy League college (not that this guarantees success and happiness in life).

As parents many of us dream of sending our kids to an Ivy League school. Never mind the kids themselves or the pressure we put on them. Is it possible that one reason we so desire these schools is that we seek to boost our own egos by having our kid labeled a "smart one" who has been accepted to an elite school?

The Ivy League schools are fine schools. So are many others. As Robert J. Samuel says in an article that appeared in *Newsweek International*, "schools don't make the student's success. Students create their own success; this makes the schools look good."

Samuel mentions a new study by Alan Krueger, an economist at Princeton, and Stacy Berg Dale, a researcher at the Andrew W. Mellon Foundation.

The outcome of their research shows that students who are prepared to make an effort can get a good education at most colleges.

The research compared the earnings of students with similar strengths, regardless of the college they went to, and found no difference.

Once the graduates enter the job market, where they studied may matter only early in their careers. A degree from an Ivy league school can impress at the beginning, but later, what matters is what they can or can't do — how they use their skills, the reputation they create, and the competence they demonstrate. In the long run these factors determine the salary they earn, regardless of the school from which they graduate.

BOTTOM LINE:

Each child is a gift, and each child is gifted in his or her own way. The only label a child should have is her or his name.

F. When wrong — I apologize

I am a human being. I make mistakes. I hope they are not too many.

We all make mistakes, and we are all entitled to make them.

At times our mistakes can hurt those on the receiving end.

Sometimes I didn't feel well. Sometimes I was tired and impatient.

I never pretended to be a supreme being or to be perfect always. I had no problem admitting my mistakes and apologizing to my girls. I did the same with my students.

If I wanted them to apologize when they were wrong, must I not have expected that of myself as well?

Who else would they learn it from?

BOTTOM LINE:

Making mistakes is human and apologizing is even more so.

G. Always keep the communication channels open

Talking about apologizing highlights the importance of communication. I can't emphasize enough the part it plays in our relationships with our kids.

At times it's not easy to communicate — in fact it can be very hard. But we have to talk and clear whatever blocks our energies and stops our relationships from flowing healthily.

We need to talk in order to move forward.

When a child misbehaves, if we say "the child is just going through a bad phase" and leave it at that, we are excusing behavior that shouldn't take place at all.

Some children are always going through "a bad phase." That doesn't entitle them to throw tantrums and do as they please whenever and wherever they feel like it.

If they are in a "bad phase" we need to talk about it. Maybe the child needs our help. Maybe the child is physically not well. Maybe the problem is with friends at school. Maybe we are the cause of the problem.

From the day my girls were born, I talked and listen to them. If we hadn't communicated, how would I have known when I was wrong? And even when I did recognize my own mistakes, how would I have corrected my wrongdoing if I hadn't been able to communicate my apologies?

When they were small and couldn't communicate with words, I "learned" and listened to their baby-language, watching their body language and decoding its meaning. I used all appropriate senses – sight, touch, smell, hearing, even common sense, in order to understand them.

Later I tuned into their verbal and non-verbal communication.

One day, when Tal was in elementary school, she came home from school, greeted me, and went straight to her room. She said nothing, but her eyes and body language made me aware that something was wrong.

I waited for her to settle down and join Orit and me for lunch. But she didn't come to the table. After a while I went to her room, where I found her lying frozen on her bed in a fetal position. I asked her how she was, and got no reply. I had never seen her behave like this before. I was worried and upset but I wasn't going to leave it, even though she didn't want to talk.

I tried to hug her, but couldn't "get in" or get close because of the way she was lying. So I sat next to her and patted her head, stroked her back, and caressed her face, all the while telling her how much I loved her.

Slowly she came out of her frozen position and let me hug her. She then started to cry. She cried her heart out while we hugged. Eventually it all came out. It was an incident that had occurred that day at school.

After she calmed down, we discussed it, and she worked out a way to handle and resolve the problem.

To this day, I still become upset when I think about the pain she endured that day for something that wasn't even her fault.

Communicating with Tal in this situation was difficult, but it was necessary — it helped her find a solution to the problem.

We should not think that we can just "press a button" and make our children communicate with us. If we want to be part of their lives, we need to communicate with them from day one.

In spite of all the warnings I received, such as "wait until your girls are in their teens, then you will see how difficult they can be," none of us noticed when they were in "that horrible, unpredictable, and unmanageable phase." We communicated as we always had, with respect, care, and trust. There was no need to rebel, and there was no one to rebel against.

Yelling, shouting, arguing, and nagging are not communication. Communicating includes the following:

— Understanding that communication is important for building our relationships with our children and building their self-esteem;

— Inviting communication so that our children know we are always willing to listen and talk about anything that is on their mind;

— Allowing children freedom of thought and expression instead of controlling their thoughts and suffocating their creativity and uniqueness;

— Accepting that we don't have to see things in the same way;

— Respecting their thoughts;

— Discussing things, not lecturing or preaching;

— Really listening and tuning in;

— Showing an interest in what children have to say;

— Letting children express their thoughts and feelings without judging, criticizing, hurting, or mocking them, all of which make children feel powerless, inadequate, and worthless and ruin their self-esteem;

— Being aware that the manner in which they are spoken, is just as important as the words we use. When we use a nasty, condescending, or cruel tone of voice, we stifle communication;

— Remembering that using "you" statements sound like attacks;

— Creating opportunities that encourage conversations, such as family meals, "dates" with a child, etc.;

— Realizing that at those times when children simply don't want to talk or wish to be alone with their thoughts, we need to respect their privacy;

— Cherishing our children's trust and not discussing their private affairs with others.

Being aware of and act on these guidelines will enable us to converse with our children and encourage them to share with us; it teaches them to verbalize and communicate.

If we create and establish solid relationship with our kids, we can communicate with them throughout their lives, no matter how young or old they may be.

If we don't talk, hoping instead that problems will disappear or somehow get solved, whatever we worry about stays there and festers. It poisons our inner being like a disease. As difficult as it may be at times, we must tackle it.

Learning to communicate within the family frame is essential for learning to communicate in general. In the home, we learn to express ourselves. If we encourage our children to talk and feel positive about verbalizing their thoughts and feelings, they will develop self-confidence and self-esteem.

In the November 1999 issue of *Vogue* Magazine, Joanne Chen writes about being shy. She says, "I hate being shy. I hate hanging out by the stereo at parties...I hate sitting in meetings, with my heart pounding, praying that my voice won't shake when it's my turn to speak." She cites research that shows how shyness and a lack of verbal skills affect the quality of our business and social lives.

Communication is the key for our interaction with people; our children need to learn, develop, and continually use these skills, both in spite of and because of the high-tech explosion surrounding us. And the starting point, as with so many other things in life, is the home!

BOTTOM LINE:

Communication is the lifeline of our relationship with our kids.

H. Guilt feelings

Some of us are brought up to feel guilty about things. Others acquire it from outside their homes. For many, it is as if we never do enough or never do well enough, or as if we do not appreciate what others do for us.

This is a dangerous and manipulative game. Children who grow up feeling that they always let us down are filled with guilt, often becoming self-destructive.

We should not bring our children up to feel guilty about us, just as we, ourselves, should not feel guilty about them.

As parents, many times we grapple with the difference between what we want to do and what we are able to do. The result is that many of us feel inadequate and guilt-ridden, because in our minds we don't match up to our own unrealistic high standards and therefore are letting our children down.

Being "the owners" of guilty feelings makes us feel worthless and weak as parents. This is like a poison that blocks our positive energy. We do not need to feel this way. It is not healthy and achieves nothing. No one benefits from it; on the contrary, we and our children stand to lose out because of it!

When we do all we can as parents out of care, thought, and love, what more can we expect of ourselves, even though our decisions are not always the best? We are only human beings!

We come to terms with our own limitations when:

— We give up the idea of being a perfect parent who has perfect children. Real people have problems, they cause problems, and they solve the problems.

— We seek, instead, to be our best and do our best.

— We accept that we do not posses a magic wand that makes everything in our children's lives pain-free and beautiful.

— We recognize that no matter what we do, our children must lead their own lives and have their own different and varied experiences, some good and others not so good.

— We realize that even our seemingly negative experiences can be valuable and, in the long run, have positive effects if we can learn from them.

— We acknowledge that it is only natural to feel bad when we make mistakes and that we need our energy for correcting what went wrong instead of wasting it on feeling guilty. We always need to move ahead.

When we make mistakes, feeling guilty cannot make things better. What improves things is solving the problem to the best of our ability and then letting it go.

To make progress we need to put futile feelings behind us.

BOTTOM LINE:

Let's focus on the present and the future instead of hanging on to the negatives of the past.

I. Leading by example

My daughters didn't gossip, because we as parents did not run down others in front of the kids or discuss with them any of the personal affairs of relatives or friends.

Some parents do talk about others in front of their kids. Sometimes these discussions are negative or private. This shows a lack of respect for others. Would any of us like to be discussed in this fashion?

Certain kids get bullied because of what other kids hear about them at home. How else would a young child become aware, for example, that another child was adopted, or born out of wedlock, or lived in a one-parent family, or differs in some respect?

Young children should never be privy to these discussions. Instead of learning to see the world through *our* prejudices, they should be taught to form their own points of view. There is plenty to talk about without meddling in other people's lives and affairs.

I never expected my daughters to behave or do something in one manner while I myself did the opposite. How many parents swear in front of their children and then punish their kids for using the same foul language that they learned from the parents in the first place?

A friend was giving her daughter of three a bath while I waited in the living room. All of a sudden I heard the child coughing terribly and screaming. I rushed to the bathroom to see what was wrong.

"It's okay," the mother told me. "She used the 'F' word, so I washed her mouth with soap. Dirty mouths should be cleaned!"

This was the act of a person who used the "F" word indiscriminately in front of everybody. Was this fair? Was it honest?

I treated my daughters the way *I wanted to be treated.*

BOTTOM LINE:

What we expect of our kids, we should first expect ourselves.

J. Creating a family structure

Only a year and a half separate Orit and Tal, but I felt that distinguishing their territories would make them feel safe and secure within the family hierarchy.

Parents have their places in the family structure, and so do the children.

Orit, who is older, received a few cents more for pocket money and was allowed to stay up later at night. As the older child, she had certain responsibilities. Tal, the younger, had hers.

This emphasized for Orit that she was the "big" child. For Tal it affirmed that she was the younger child. Each felt "important" because of her unique position.

Each child within a family is unique. Each is different. Each has individual character, strengths, weaknesses, and needs.

There are many reasons for these differences. Gender, birth order, age and constitution, all make children unique. Our dealings with our children and our relationships with them must be different. Each child has to be handled differently. We need to tune in to their personal beings and discover their individual strengths.

We must be fair and pay attention to each child. Because kids have different personalities and needs, they should not be treated identically.

We need to devote focused, separate time to the child, going out on "dates," for example, with each child. I used to do it often with my daughters. We would go to a restaurant, an ice-cream parlor, a bookshop, whatever we chose.

Our dates gave us opportunities to connect and enabled me to make each child feel important and special. These were adventures alone with her mother, with no sharing. And I never let them down — once we made a date, out we went!

We want our kids to grow up as our friends, not our enemies. One way to achieve this is by not making them jealous of one another. Sharing time alone with each child makes each one feel appreciated and loved.

Although I have two daughters who are close in age, I hardly ever bought them the same clothes or dressed them the same. I encouraged them to chose their own clothes at the store, limiting them only by budget and their needs. I wanted them to develop their own tastes and personal styles and to learn to decide for themselves. Today, when they look at some of the photos we have, they laugh at the way they dressed themselves. I smile too. But it's okay. They wore then what they liked and what they felt comfortable with — that's what counted.

BOTTOM LINE:

Parents and children have their own unique places in the family hierarchy

K. Demonstrating my love and care

Our children's self-esteem results directly from the way we treat them. Giving them a sense of feeling lovable and capable is the strongest foundation we can create for solving the future challenges of their lives. The ideal is for them to develop a healthy self-esteem and self-confidence, regardless of what others may think about them.

Our children's self-esteem develops because of the quality of our relationships with them. When they feel loved, they understand that they are worthy of being loved, and they develop a self-esteem that governs all areas of their lives.

Children who believe that they are worthy, capable, accepted, loved, and important are satisfied and happy to be themselves. This positive view of themselves shapes all their actions.

We all need to know that we are worthy and loved. We need to see, feel, and hear it.

I made sure that Orit and Tal always remembered that they were loved. I communicated it verbally simply by telling them that I loved them. I physically hugged, caressed, and embraced them. And I did special projects with them and for them.

I enjoy demonstrating my love to my ladies, no less than they enjoy being on the receiving end.

BOTTOM LINE:

Our children always need to know and feel that they are loved.

16.
MOTHERHOOD IS NOT A
REHEARSAL — IT'S THE REAL THING

Some of us complain...

— No one taught us how to be parents;

— All our problems are the fault of our parents;

—Our parents didn't understand us, didn't communicate with us, made us feel guilty, didn't really care, weren't there when we needed them...

But, where did our parents learn to become parents?

Who taught them?

We are mature adults when we take responsibility for our lives and for what happens to us. We stop blaming others and move on.

There comes a point in our lives when we have to cut the umbilical cord and stand up for what we believe in. Becoming parents is the greatest responsibility we will ever have. It is our chance to do the right things with our kids and, in a way, correct all the things for which we blame our parents.

Over the years, I have met quite a few people, women and men, who were bitter about their parents. They resented them and blamed them for every problem they faced in their lives. It may have been far from reality, but it was a convenient crutch, an excuse for failure.

The irony is that *their* children often talked critically about *them* as parents, describing them as lousy and neglectful.

It is easy to criticize our parents. The more important question is, what do we do when we embark on the path of parenthood? How do we better and improve things?

We cannot keep on playing blaming games while we forget the real issue at hand: the well being of our children. If we wanted to play these games, why have children who in turn will blame us? When does this Catch-22 end?

Merely having children doesn't make a woman a mother, just as having a stethoscope doesn't turn a person into a doctor. Motherhood is the most important and demanding professional career a woman can have. The on-the-job training never ends.

From the moment I decided to become a mother, I took full responsibility for the lives of my future children. It had nothing to do with my parents and everything to do with Terry and me.

— Any mistake I made was my mistake, not my parents.

— Anything I messed up was my fault, not my parents

I never blamed my parents for my actions or my inactions. Only I was responsible. When I was wrong, I apologized and made sure I learned from the experience so I didn't repeat it.

At the beginning of the book *Anna Karenina*, Tolstoy says, "All happy families resemble one another, but each unhappy family is unhappy in its own way."

In spite of our personal and individual differences, as parents we all want to achieve the same thing: the happiness of our children and our family. Instead of being unique in our unhappiness and blaming our parents for it, let's consciously change what we faulted them for. Let's make sure that our children learn from us the right way to be parents and to create happy families that resemble one another in their happiness.

BOTTOM LINE:

Let's become personally aware about the things that we should do now to improve our effectiveness as parents.

17.
ORIT'S VIEW

Before we get into the "bottom lines" of motherhood, I would like to express some personal thoughts.

I am starting a new family. I am excited about bringing a new life into this world, and I am nervous. I am more aware of child-parent relationships. And seeing that I am in the "training and coaching" field, I am acutely aware of how parents communicate with their children and how children test the boundaries set by their parents.

Unfortunately it isn't all that encouraging.

I often notice the lack of respect that many children have for their parents and how little real power parents have.

By real power I mean respect, trust, and authority that are earned (not forced) through the strength and love that parents demonstrate.

Real power also means that the parents' word is their bond. What they say and do has tremendous value. Parents are not "push-overs." If they say, "no," it means just that and they need to say it only once.

I grew up with parents who have real power.

Imagine a typical family going away for a vacation. They travel in their S.U.V. The parents sit in front, the father listening to the radio, the mother talking to a friend on the cell phone. The kids in the back listen to their CD-players with headphones.

And so starts the vacation!

This is incomprehensible to me, and yet it's the norm today.

In the past, when I dared say something, I commonly heard people say: "Wait, Orit, until you have kids then you'll see." I also often hear: "Kids are a lot of work."

These remarks, which are often said in front of the children, sound so ominous to me. I ask myself, "Why does anyone have kids willingly if it is so hard? Why go through it?" I don't understand this!

I never heard my parents make comments such as these. I would have been hurt if they did. What I heard was that my sister and I were a huge bonus and an added joy to their lives, not "work."

What I realize now, more than ever before, is that my mom has insights into motherhood that are incredibly evolved.

I don't know where she learnt to be so wise and downright smart about raising confident, happy, independent, and balanced daughters. She just "has it."

I want to duplicate my experience with my mom

with my own children. If I can do even half as good a job —
I will have done well !

I think that other mothers will benefit from what she
knows.

My father played a congruent and huge role in the
development and upbringing of my sister and me. But since
this book is on "motherhood" specifically, let me focus on
my mother's attitude and awareness.

When I ask myself, "what does Noya have that makes
her an outstanding mother beside her care and love?" I
immediately think of integrity, assertiveness, empathy,
trust, strength, privacy, fairness, and non-competitiveness.

Integrity

Noya is one of the most reliable, trustworthy people I
have ever met. Her word is her bond. Once she says she
will do something, you can consider it done, and she does
it way ahead of schedule. If she promises, she will always
deliver.

She expects the same from us. If my sister and I say
that we will do something, it is expected we will do it, no
matter what ... no excuses.

I felt so lucky when I was a little girl. I was so grateful
that my mom, who worked, was always on time to pick me
and other kids up from ballet, tennis, drama, and any other
of our activities. I remember how upset some of my peers
used to be when their moms were late or forgot to pick us
up altogether!

My mom was never late ... ever! Imagine that! If my
mom said, "Girls, tomorrow we are going to see a movie,"

we would see the movie the next day. When the next day came, we'd never hear, "Oh, I don't feel like it," or "Something's come up, let's do it another time." That didn't happen with the "small things" in our lives and for sure not with the more serious ones.

There was no confusion. Everything was clear and straightforward, and we always knew were we stood.

Assertiveness

Oh yes! This lady knows how to say "no," and she does it in a respectful manner.

If she wasn't prepared to do something, she would say so. We used to get upset sometimes and ask "why?" We would then get an answer, forget about the "no," and move on. She talked to us, explained her decisions, and generally spoke in a very adult way. She never treated us like little kids. She talked to us with respect in her voice and dignity in her manner.

I respected my mom even more for having the strength to say "no" rather than trying to be nice and say "yes," which later became "no."

Empathy

This characteristic is essential. My mom is one of those rare people who truly sees and feels things from our perspective. She could often feel the pain we experienced at various stages in our lives and connect with us on that level. She always was my greatest confidante, someone I could talk to about anything.

Trust

We always trusted each other. Tal and I fully trusted Noya, and she trusted us, to follow through on anything that we were supposed to do.

Knowing that she trusted us made us feel appreciated, respected, and responsible. She always assumed the best of us and always had positive visions of where we would go in life and who we could become. She expected the best in a "non-pushy" way.

Noya believed we would do the very best we could — for ourselves, not for her. We did just that, the very best we could!

Strength

Noya is a strong person. She is tough and will not allow others to hurt her or her family. She can be fierce if there is a threat to anyone in the family. I remember her confronting teachers on occasion when she felt that an injustice had been done to us and that we couldn't handle it ourselves.

When an art teacher once told my sister that she had no talent and should not pursue art in the future, my mother had a "chat" with the teacher and gave her a piece of her mind.

She knew that my sister dreamed about a career in art and believed in her ability. She stood behind her child all the way.

My sister now has a Master of Fine Arts degree. She has won top prizes for her creative achievements as a student in Europe and the United States. She now works in the entertainment industry as a lighting designer, a very artistic field.

I credit much of my sister's success to my mom's strength, encouragement, and backing. She would not just lie down and say, "Oh well."

Privacy

Noya never discussed our problems with her friends and acquaintances. She would share her concerns with my father, and that was it.

I know that many parents openly discuss personal issues concerning their kids with others.

I would have been so upset if my mother ever did that to me! It would have betrayed my confidence. I wouldn't have trusted her and would have been very careful about what I told her.

She was also very "modest" about our successes. She didn't show off how great we were. It was private, and she was quiet about that, too.

Fairness

Neither my sister nor I ever felt that mom preferred one over the other. She would not get involved in sibling squabbles. She would simply say, " Please don't make me judge and state who is right and who is wrong. That could be unfair and might create more problems if I looked as if I sided with one of you against the other. Each one of you has her own perception of what your 'issue' is about, so go ahead and sort it out by yourselves."

I look back at this insight of hers, and I think it was

very powerful. My sister and I learned how to resolve conflicts amicably from a young age.

Non-competitiveness

Noya has never competed with other people or parents. She cares about a person's quality as a human being. But she is not curious or concerned about someone else's financial situation, where they are traveling to, where they live, or what they drive.

We were not even aware of "jealousy" until we were much older, when we learned about it from listening to and watching others. We were taught that if we competed, we competed with ourselves, that we compared ourselves to our previous best record, not anyone else's.

We were successful if we improved ourselves, not if we got better grades than someone else or became better ballet dancers or tennis players than they.

We felt no pressure to win against others. This non-competitive philosophy allowed me to develop a solid self-esteem. I was encouraged to set my own standards, and I felt trusted to live up to them.

Communication skills

Noya talked to us as if we were adults, from day one. She talked to us when she was pregnant, when we were infants, and ever since.

She made us part of everything by always including us, even as babies sitting in the high chair, flinging food all over the place.

If she was upset about something, she didn't steam and simmer but let us know immediately. Nothing got "swept under the rug." She did this in a way that allowed us to maintain our dignity and self-respect.

When she was wrong, she admitted it and apologized. Everything was dealt with; the communication was always clear and never blocked.

At times the issues were not easy to deal with, but my gutsy mother would tackle them. She would not allow "weird vibes" to float around our house for too long.

Educator

Education was always a top priority for Noya. Nothing was more important since our early years. She encouraged us to study and pursue occupations that were interesting, creative, and financially liberating.

My sister has a Master of Arts degree and is a lightening designer in the entertainment world. I too have a Master's degree, and am following in my father's steps. I am a trainer and a coach in the business world. Both our occupations are challenging, creative, and financially rewarding.

There were always books around the house, including a wonderful set of encyclopedias that I used extensively until I was in the eighth grade.

During elementary school, I never had to go to the library for school assignments, because our house was one huge library.

Learning was fun. Noya was a university lecturer and was always busy reading. She taught us to be independent and to look up the answers to the millions of questions we had about everything. She said, "I don't know the answers to all your questions, but I know where you can find them. Let me show you." She showed us how to look up information, and away we went, feeling a great sense of achievement for being so independent.

Noya and Terry believed in the power of travel to educate their children. They included us in most of their international travel, even when we were very young. They would book a trip, pay it off during the year, and once it was paid for, book a new trip.

By traveling together we bonded as a family, enriched the experience for each other, and learned about the world. My father has said that those international trips we took as a family were some of the happiest memories he has of his life.

We grew up aware of cultural differences and felt comfortable in different environments.

After each trip I would read the history of the places and people we visited. I would look it up in the atlas. I would read stories from that country and listen to the music of composers from these countries. After visiting these places, I wanted to know more about their people and culture.

I remember each trip so vividly! To this day, my parents call on me to remind them of where we were in a particular year, and what we saw. Don't listen to people when they say that travel is wasted on children. It was a huge bonus in our lives, and it gave us an evolved and unique perspective of the world.

*****

The uniqueness of this book is that it is not just theory.

It is not a preaching to *others* what *they* should do. It comes from personal experience; whatever my mother talks about was and is her experience.

My sister and I are grateful for the opportunity to share our thoughts and feelings. We wish her to be a mentoring mother to us and to others.

18.
TAL'S VIEW

Dear Mom,

I know it has taken me a long time to sit down and write this piece.

At first, when I said that I would add my input to this book, I thought it would be no problem. I mean, how hard could it be to tell the world that *in my eyes* I have the perfect mother?

But when it came down to the actual act, I realized that explaining why you are the perfect mother is something I have difficulty describing in words.

To me, you are the perfect mother, because you have always treated me with respect, as a human being. Every thought, opinion, or comment I had as a child was valid. You never talked down to me. When I needed you to be my friend, my mom, you were there. When I needed you to be my mommy, you were there to wipe my tears, give me a hug, or stroke my hair. No matter how old or what the situation, I always felt better when you did that thing of gently stroking my eyebrows. It always has been and always will be comforting to me.

You are the perfect mother because you never did my schoolwork for me, encouraging me instead to find the answers in books and research. You sat for hours studying with me until you too knew how photosynthesis worked and how long it took the red train to move to point A and the blue train to move to point B at heavens knows what speed and who really needs to know the answer? But you helped me figure it out, knowing that the process of figuring it out was more important than the answer itself.

You showed your interest in my life at school to my teachers and at college to my professors. You supported me in every extracurricular activity. No matter how bad an actress I was, I could see Academy Awards in your eyes. If I did gymnastics, I was worthy of a gold medal in your heart (even if I couldn't pull myself over the uneven bars). But you never made me feel pressure to be an achiever. You never pushed me to do anything.

You were not an overbearing mother on the sidelines. But you were there, cheering, supporting, and being my mom.

You gave me the freedom to be social, always assuring me of your trust in me to make the right decisions. You were and are always loyal, disliking anyone who hurts me and loving those who are good to me.

Mom, for all the things I have written in this letter, there are thousands more.

How could I ever put this love and friendship you've shown me into words? You and dad made me into the person I am today. I am a best friend, I am a wife, I have a career, and I have the perfect mother.

I can only wish to be a fraction of the human being you are. I promise to pass the love you have given me on to my children.

I love you!
Tal

19.
SUMMARY

1. "What you write, is what you actually did, and we know that it works — it worked for us. And maybe others will also enjoy reading your thoughts." — Orit and Tal.

2. When we are ready to become mothers and parents, we need to understand why we want children in our lives and that we are taking on a lifetime commitment.

3. As role models we respect our "selves" and value the "selves" of our children.

4. Instead of using negative language when talking about bringing up our children, let's rather focus on the joy this creativity brings to our marriage and our lives.

5. Let's allow and encourage our children to dream and chase their own rainbows.

6. Treat our children as unique individuals without comparing them to others.

7. Both parents must consider a child's requests with respect and empathy, regardless of how mundane the requests might be.

To avoid and prevent conflicts, we should always ask ourselves the following:

— If I were a child now, would I want to be treated this way?

— When I was a child, was I happy when my parents treated me in this manner?

— How did I want to be treated?

8. Stick with our decisions and follow through with them.

9. We are responsible for bringing up responsible children.

10. Spoiled brats are created by their parents.

11. We create mutual trust between our children and ourselves by modeling it ourselves.

12. Punishment is a serious statement that should educate our children, not hurt or damage them.

13. We must always be there for our kids and take full responsibility for the outcome.

14. Out of respect, our parents do not take away our responsibility to our children. Out of respect, we do not impose our parental responsibility on our parents.

15. Becoming a mother is no reason for self-neglect.

16. We don't fish for the kids; we teach them how to fish.

17. The word "boredom" doesn't appear in our vocabulary.

18. Our children are part of the family and should be made to feel that way.

19. Each child is a gift, and each child is gifted in his or her own way. The only label a child should have is her or his name.

20. Making mistakes is human and apologizing is even more so.

21. Communication is the lifeline of our relationship with our kids.

22. Let's focus on the present and the future instead of hanging on to the negatives of the past.

23. What we expect of our kids, we should first expect of ourselves.

24. Parents and children have their own unique places in the family hierarchy.

25. Our children always need to know and feel that they are loved.

26. Let's become personally aware about the things that we should do now to improve our effectiveness as parents.

* * *

Below are some questions we can use as reminders for ourselves. We can tailor-make them for our individual needs.

CHECK LIST

<u>Before our child is born</u>

A. Do my husband and I want a child?

B. Do we know why?

C. Are we ready to be parents?

D. Do we understand that this is a commitment and responsibility for life?

<u>From the birth of our child onward</u>

A. What did I want as a daughter? Now that I am a mother, do I give that to my child?

B. Do I enrich my life as a person so that I keep on growing instead of feeling that I am wasting my life?

C. Do I spend enough time with my child?

D. How is my communication with my child?

E. Am I "firm and fair" with each child individually?

F. Am I fair, not preferring one child to the other and therefore not encouraging sibling jealousy?

G. Am I there to encourage and support?

H. Does my child feel respected and trusted?

I. Do I hug, kiss, and touch my child?

J. Am I a role model? Do I do what I expect?

K. Do I remember the following?

— No name calling;

— No comparison to others;

— The child is the parents' full responsibility;

— It is human to make mistakes and to apologize.

L. Do I accept that my child and I are "only" human beings and therefore imperfect?

M. Do my husband and I enjoy being parents?

* * *

Life is an ongoing process and a "happening."

As time passes, changes occur and our relationships change too. We have to be flexible, adaptable, and open-minded.

As we move on, we may have to change or re-negotiate the codes and rules in the relationships we create with our kids. What was right for a child of five is different when that child is fifteen, eighteen, or twenty-one.

Thanks to technological change, each generation of parents has to cope with different challenges. We are not machines. Our basic human needs remain the same and ought be addressed. Children who use the Internet and communicate via e-mails need as much love, care, respect, and trust as their parents and grandparents did when they were kids.

What I describe and discuss in this book was and still is my way. It is a personal approach made up of my own ingredients. It is not a research document. Each family is a different and unique entity. Each family has its own special dynamic created by the people involved in that particular family.

All that really counts is that parents and children alike feel happy about the relationships within the family.

BOTTOM LINE:

There are no perfect parents
There are no perfect children
Our children are the future
Motherhood isn't funny, but it's great fun!